UNVEILING TRUTH
God and His Children

KATERYANN JOHNSON, CPA, CGMA, CFF

authorHOUSE®

AuthorHouse™
1663 Liberty Drive
Bloomington, IN 47403
www.authorhouse.com
Phone: 1 (800) 839-8640

Edited by Pastor Peter Lanya

King James Version (KJV)
Public Domain

Amplified Bible (AMP)
Copyright © 2015 by The Lockman Foundation, La
Habra, CA 90631. All rights reserved.

New King James Version (NKJV)
Scripture taken from the New King James Version®. Copyright © 1982
by Thomas Nelson. Used by permission. All rights reserved.

New International Version (NIV)
Holy Bible, New International Version®, NIV® Copyright ©1973, 1978, 1984,
2011 by Biblica, Inc.® Used by permission. All rights reserved worldwide.

Published by AuthorHouse 01/28/2017

ISBN: 978-1-5246-5944-8 (sc)
ISBN: 978-1-5246-5943-1 (e)

Print information available on the last page.

Any people depicted in stock imagery provided by Thinkstock are models,
and such images are being used for illustrative purposes only.
Certain stock imagery © Thinkstock.

This book is printed on acid-free paper.

 Prophetic Ambassador Kateryann Johnson also called Minister Kay was born and grew up in the beautiful island of Nassau, Bahamas. She is the excited mother of two boys, S.J. and K'Juan.

Recognizing the call of God on her life to preach, thus having been asked by other prominent and anointed men of God (nationally and internationally) to speak at conferences and church engagements began the manifestation of the powerful gift that is in this powerful vessel. The Spirit of the Lord is upon her and she has been anointed to preach the gospel. She is a life coach and a prolific, empowerment preacher.

She has many academic accolades. She is a CPA by profession with both CGMA and CFF credentials. Moreover, she has a degree in Theology. But more importantly, she is an anointed and mighty woman of God who is grounded in the Word of God and led by the Spirit of God. She is the talk show host of Echo Chamber Live aired in the Bahamas.

Prophetess Kay is the founder of Prophetic Evangelism Network. Moreover, she is the author of the books called In Pursuit Prayer and Devotional Journal, Unlocking the Financial Gate, Heart of a Worshiper and Unveiling Truth. She is greatly anticipating the release of a few more books. She has a unique gift for imparting the prophetic understanding of times and seasons with a message of preparation and expectancy.

She is marveled by what God is doing in her life. She has been mandated by God to assist in the restoration of the five fold ministry found in Eph. 4:11 to help get the bride, the church ready for the day of the saints and the return of Jesus Christ.

Her life has been shaped based on Jeremiah 29:11.

DEDICATION

This book is dedicated to God and my two precious, handsome sons who I affectionately call SJ and K'Juan. I have already declared that their souls have been preserved for the Kingdom of God and their lives shall bring my God glory in Jesus name.

TABLE OF CONTENTS

INTRODUCTION

Over the years, I have met countless people both in the church and in the world with one thing in the mind - SUCCESS. They want success in their career, success in ministry, success in marriage, success in their children, success in their business and some success at their place of work. Success seems to be a word that is found upon people's lips every now and then. Shockingly, the records show not all people succeed. Some people try to success through thick and thin, but they do not make ends meet. Others try and it seems like success smiles at them like a baby who has learned how to speak.

Everything has a price. And as they say, the end justifies the means. Successful people pay a high price to realize their achievements whereas failures attempt once and leave if it fails. In this book, you will encounter the process successful people have used to reach where they are. We learn from people, so be humble and willing to receive instructions that I believe will help you in life.

It is good people that want success, victory and promotion which are the best things in life. But remember, there is a process to go through. Sometimes, the process is not good. It may involve a lot of pain, waiting, loneliness and rejection. Those who stand the test will celebrate at the end. Joseph, Moses, Abraham and many other seasoned men and women of God recorded in the Bible, went through tough times. It was not smooth. They dared their fears, confronted their challenges and believed God to move in their favor. Hebrews records their experiences as heroes of faith because they endured the pain and came out as a testimony. What you survive from and your experiences are testimonies to others. People see you as a model to emulate and a living testimony to help them move forward in life.

You may wonder now at yourself as you feel the pain and the heat of the trials you are currently facing. You look around to see who is standing with you, but you see nobody there. Friends have deserted you. The conditions around you is tense and in a sorrowful state. At this time, the devil is mocking at you that God has left you and he goes on to whisper in your ears, "You are a failure". When you look at yourself, your pain is growing bigger and bigger by the day. The power to hold on is diminishing at high speed. What you see ahead is darkness and gloomy picture. You pray and fast, but to no avail. The last option is to give up and give in your resignation letter. You want to call it quits and forget that you ever lived.

I want to encourage you, there is always light at the end of the tunnel. Inside your pain, there is sweetness, light dawns after darkness has receded in the background, and after the sunshine there is rain again to begin a new season. So, no condition is permanent. Everything comes and goes. You are connected to a destiny that holds the promise and hope of many people. You have notions in your loins. So, if you do not move expeditiously, those people depending on you will lose their way. See beyond where you are and hold tightly on the promises of God. God can never fail you; His Word for you will come to pass.

God is saying to you, "1 am about to open a new page for you. Don't give up. Your season of mourning has come to an end, behold 1 am doing a new thing for you".

Isaiah 43:18-19--"Do not remember the former things, nor consider the things of old. Behold, I will do a new thing, now it shall spring forth; shall you not know it? I will even make a road in the wilderness andrivers in the desert--NKJV

In this book, l will show why you need to persevere in your trials, temptations and pain in order to secure your destiny. God has promised you, of course, good things and a fulfilled destiny, but there is a process to go through. You must accept the process before you are given what has been promised. Many people, especially believers, want the best from God, but they are not ready for the process. Remember, process determines the end-product. The enemy cannot stop what God has made in the fiery furnace. It will stand the tests of time.

Go with me in this timely book to encourage you and inspire you towards your destiny.

CHAPTER 1

THE IMPORTANCE OF SACRIFICE

After reading stories of successful people in books and the Bible, I have come to the conclusion that sacrifice ushers you to the next level. Sacrifice, whichever form it takes, is a pre-requisite for success in life. And I, honestly, think it is impossible to succeed without first taking a step of risk. Or let me just say, the more sacrifices you do, the more successful you would become.

I honestly don't know what you are going through, but I know that your current challenges are going to lead you to the land of champions. You need to sacrifice. The paths of least resistance goes nowhere. It only ends in regrets, failures and stagnation.

When you read through the Bible, you notice characters like Joseph, David, Abraham and so many others who overcame and took a step of sacrifice to attain their promises. When you look at the story of the young man-Joseph, you will notice that sacrifice truly prepares you for success. From the adversity in his family (after he revealed his dream to them) to the pit from which he was sold to the Ishmaelites as well as the temptations he faced in Potiphar's house to the Prison and finally to the Palace (with Pharaoh), Joseph's life is a real study of sacrifice. He had all the reasons to forget about his family, but he remembered them. He forgot about the past and took a risk to invite them into Egypt.

What sacrifice have you done to others?

The church is where it is because people have refused sacrifice to move to the next level. If you continue to tolerate your conditions, you won't change them. Sacrifice is the step you need to take to leave your present conditions and create what you desire.

If there is no sacrifice, there is no power. Power comes when you lay down your life for a cause. Look at Jesus; He sacrificed His life for us, now we have power to become the sons of God.

John 1:12--But as many as received him, to them gave he power to become the sons of God, [even] to them that believe on his name--KJV

Aside Joseph, David's life illustrates the fact that sacrifice prepares you for success. From working as Saul's musician to facing Goliath to escaping from Saul's murder attempts to being anointed as King of Judah, David's life is a real study in sacrifice. He had all the reasons to live a life of ease. Any army that is at ease can become a casualty. You need to be alert always to override the schemes of the enemy. This comes by sacrifice. So, your attitude towards sacrifice needs to change

Start seeing sacrifice as the ladder to climb to your promised land of success. See sacrifice as a tool the enemy will try to use to stop you from doing. You must contend with him. For every new level in life, there is a new devil to contend with. So, be prepared for it, welcome it with open arms. If you're able to overcome, moving to the next level becomes mince meat. In my life, I can also testify to the fact that sacrifice prepares you for success.

Every time I have moved a step higher in life, I've had to sacrifice equal to the new level. If you are the type that does not want feathers ruffled, you just like peace and tranquility, you are not ready for success. You must be prepared to shake things and situations around you. Do not forget that the definition of insanity is doing things the same way and expecting a different result. To those who are tired of status quo, are the people willing to sacrifice for something better.

Like Apostle Paul, they say,"Philippians 3:13-14

Brethren, I count not myself to have apprehended: but [this] one thing [I do], forgetting those things which are behind, and reaching forth unto those things which are before, I press toward the mark for the prize of the high calling of God in Christ Jesus.(KJV)

Friends, the key to your next level is sacrifice. The enemy won't agree with you to move, he will try every gimmicks to keep you in the same level. Progress calls for sacrifice. Ministry is sacrifice. What about marriage, without sacrifice it ends up as a formality where two people agrees to live together to pass time. God send his son, Jesus, as a sacrifice to the world. We are born again and washed by the blood because somebody paid the price. Somebody may ask me, "why should we pay the price yet Jesus did?" That is a good question. Let me say this in simplicity, "balanced diet ensures healthy body. Spiritual exercises like prayer, giving, reading God's word and fellowship with other believers makes you strong. There are certain levels in life you can only attain through sacrifice. Jesus paid for us not to be lazy and irresponsible. Wake up from slumber and redeem your time because the days are evil.

From henceforth let no man trouble me: for I bear in my body the marks of the Lord Jesus. Brethren, the grace of our Lord Jesus Christ [be] with your spirit-- Galatians 6:17-18, KJV

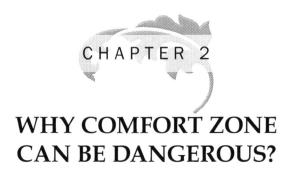

CHAPTER 2

WHY COMFORT ZONE
CAN BE DANGEROUS?

Instead of taking the leap, we make reasons for staying in our comfort zones.

** I wanted to grow my business, but did not want to invest or take a risk.
** I wanted to travel, but was waiting until I had the money or time.
** I wanted to see my family more often, but was so busy with my business.
** I wanted my marriage to improve, but would not spend the money on therapy.

Comfort zone is the killer disease to productivity. Staying at the same place for a long time is dangerous. It kills creativity, diligence and even your vision can die gradually.

The LORD our God spake unto us in Horeb, saying, Ye have dwelt long enough in this mount: Turn you, and take your journey, and go to the mount of the Amorites, and unto all [the places] nigh thereunto, in the plain, in the hills, and in the vale, and in the south, and by the sea side, to the land of the Canaanites, and unto Lebanon, unto the great river, the river Euphrates. Behold,

I have set the land before you: go in and possess the land which the LORD sware unto your fathers, Abraham, Isaac, and Jacob, to give unto them and to their seed after them-- Deuteronomy 1:6-8, KJV

I hear God is saying to you, you have stayed there too long. It is now time to break camp and move to the next level.

God told the children of Israel to come out of their comfort zone and go in to possess the land. You cannot possess your inheritance in the comfort zone. It is time to arise. I see you taking your possessions. Go in and occupy.

The Danger of the Comfort Zone

The COMFORT ZONE is a state of mind where you do not feel the need of challenging yourself. You follow the flow of events of your days, managing to handle things as they go. But you never really put yourself in a risky position. You are not willing to take any sacrifice.

The comfort zone is a behavioral state within which a person operates in an anxiety-neutral condition, using a limited set of behaviors to deliver a steady level of performance, usually without a sense of risk.

I suppose this is a very natural thing and I believe we all tend to fall in our comfort zone as time goes.

If you do not step out from your comfort zone, soon enough you'll stop challenging yourself. You'll be in a sort of autopilot mode where things get done without too much pain. Eventually, you'll stop learning new things and one day you will wake up and realize that you're bored. You must leave the comfort zone. There is too much to lose.

That is the danger in getting trapped by your own ability to initiate changes you need by not willing to put in sacrifice.

The risk you pay when you step out is the price to gain. You would have more experience, become stronger at what you do and maybe have access to another level of achievement.

Stepping out of the comfort zone raises the anxiety level engendering a stress response. The result is an enhanced level of concentration and focus.

Your Comfort Zone is The Danger Zone!

The greatest obstacle to success is complacency – being in your comfort zone. Highly successful people will tell you that the secret to their success was doing what was uncomfortable. They were prepared, actually eager, to make the sacrifices necessary to achieve success.

Thomas Edison said, *"We shall have no better conditions in the future if we are satisfied with all those which we have at present."*

Sacrifice is the name given to a person who is willing to lose something in life. There is danger of staying in your comfort zone. The children of Israel preferred to go back to Egypt, their comfort zone, that is why they murmured every time they faced a setback. God did not spare them; they all died in the wilderness except those who were willing to go forward.

Reasons Why Comfort Zone is Dangerous

2 Kings 7:3-7 (AMP) -Now four men who were lepers were at the entrance of the city's gate; and they said to one another, Why do we sit here until we die?

If we say, we will enter the city — then the famine is in the city, and we shall die there; and if we sit still here, we die also. So now come, let us go over to the army of the Syrians. If they spare us alive, we shall live; and if they kill us, we shall but die.

So they arose in the twilight and went to the Syrian camp. But when they came to the edge of the camp, no man was there.

For the Lord had made the Syrian army hear a noise of chariots and horses, the noise of a great army. They had said to one another, The king of Israel has hired the Hittite and Egyptian kings to come upon us.

So the Syrians arose and fled in the twilight and left their tents, horses, donkeys, even the camp as it was, and fled for their lives.

The four lepers were comfortable, yet suffering and in pain. They were rejected and cast outside the city to die gradually. No leper could be allowed to mingle with others. That was the method of dealing with lepers, ostracize them from other people.

But the four lepers made a decision to come out of such a situation. They dared to face their enemies of life that is fear, rejection and sympathy. When they took the journey to face the physical enemy, the battle had already been decided to their favor. Understand this friend; the real enemy of our life is within. **When you conquer the internal enemy, the outside enemy falls apart**. The lepers who were rejected became celebrities in the land. Your success, profits, wedding, ministry or business is not found in the comfortable zones. Make a decision today to begin the journey of unknown, the unfamiliar and untested ground that hides your true blessings.

When somebody approaches me and ask me this question,

"How can I acquire what I want and succeed in life?"

I answer back,

"Do something out of your normal routine and start thinking outside the box. Be willing to sacrifice".

In order to achieve the success that you want, you must be able to think and act outside the normal comfort zone. This is why Apple changed the game in computer technology, Manny Pacquiao became the world's greatest boxer and Mark Zuckerberg became the youngest billionaire by creating Facebook.

In situations where I talk to somebody who wants to create change and success in their life, but aren't willing to be outside their comfort zone, I remember what Albert Einstein had said,

Insanity is doing the same things over and over again, expecting different results.

Most people who have achieved their goals in life and are successful in what they do, had gone through situations where they have risked themselves and be out of their comfort zone. Because you cannot change your circumstance by doing the same things, you have to think and act outside your normal routine in order to achieve different result.

Let us look at these dangers of staying in the comfort zones:

1. **Comfort Zone Blocks Growth**
2. **Comfort Zone Drives You Down to Hardship**
3. **Comfort Zone Leads to Boredom and Discontentment**
4. **Comfort Zone Triggers Negative Mindset -** An idle mind is the devil's playground.
5. **Comfort Zone Causes Lack of Drive and Purpose**
6. **Comfort Zone Leads to Missed Opportunity**
7. **Comfort Zone Limits Chance to Live Life to its Fullest**

Personally, I have experienced a stage where I have taken risk and went out of my comfort zone. When I did it, I have encountered a lot of negative sayings and judgment. But that did not stop me from moving out of my comfort zone and pursue my purpose. It is the time when so many positive changes happened in my life and the moment when my dream turned into reality.

When God called me into the ministry and I stepped out, people did not believe me. They saw my decision as badly timed, foolishness and will lead to more hardships. I did not believe them because I remained focused to my calling and now it is speaking. People who were mocking me then, are now celebrating me.

Now it came to pass, when Sanballat, and Tobiah, and Geshem the Arabian, and the rest of our enemies, heard that I had builded the wall, and [that] there was no breach left therein; (though at that time I had not set up the doors upon the gates;) That Sanballat and Geshem sent unto me, saying, Come, let us meet together in [some one of] the villages in the plain of Ono. But they thought to do me mischief. And I sent messengers unto them, saying, I [am] doing a great work, so that I cannot come down: why should the work cease, whilst I leave it, and come down to you? Yet they sent unto me four times after this sort; and I answered them after the same manner- Nehemiah 6:1-4, KJV

9

Nehemiah faced stiff opposition when he decided to rebuild the walls of Jerusalem. The enemies tried all means to stop him but in vain. Then, later, they wanted to distract him from the vision, Nehemiah stuck to the vision.

"I am doing a great work, why should I come down?"

Remain focused. Keep pressing on and fulfill your assignment.

Remember this:

We cannot become what we want to be by remaining what we are. We can only change our life, if we are brave enough to be out of our comfort zone. Because the first step to change in your circumstances is a change from within you.

CHAPTER 3

ACCEPT DIVINE TESTING BEFORE PROMOTION

Divine destiny is the place where the script of life is formed; the place where God designed us to become.That place may not be smooth and easy sailing as you think. Sometimes it brings discomfort and makes us nervous. Comfort zones can be a deathbed to your destiny. Everyone has a comfort zone. People feel good in comfort areas. They are used to the same things because they are familiar. Unfamiliar ground and people make us nervous. But it is in these areas that people grow. New things challenge our faith and cause us to develop further. Never fear uncommon grounds.

Divine destiny may take you to uncommon grounds. Your faith must be tested before you receive your promotion. Understand God always takes us away from comfort zone. He separates us from familiar people and environment to make us become better. He wants us to trust in Him alone. In this environment, God receives all the glory because it was impossible according to the eyes of people. Abraham was separated. Elijah and Elisha were separated. David was separated and God began molding him to become a king. Apostle Paul was also separated. Jesus, the son of God, was separated from familiar grounds and taken to the wilderness for preparation and equipping.

God's plans are good and wonderful, but sometimes they lead us to the place of testing and discomfort. That is why God may shake you from your cocoon to take you in unfamiliar areas to develop you for His glory. Eagles take out their eaglets in a flight school away from the nest. You cannot develop spiritual muscles in a bed of roses. You need to burn bridges and break camp in order to move to another level. God's plan may take you in an unfamiliar zone where you faith is tested. Be willing to move as God moves to new realms in the spirit.

Jeremiah 29:11--For I know the thoughts that I think toward you, says the LORD, thoughts of peace and not of evil, to give you a future and a hope—NKJV

Most people want glory without going through testing. They want promotion without pain. They want prosperity without the value of labor. Nothing good comes on a silver plate.

When there's a shift in our life, we should discern the plan of God. Our security is to know that God understands our destiny and we are ready to move with Him. Transitions ordained by God take place in our life and we cannot avoid them. A case and point is the encounter Jacob had. God changed Jacob's name into Israel which means "The Prince of God'" before He fulfilled his destiny. Jacob was ready to go through his transitions. Not all transitions are good; sometimes you go through loneliness, pain and discomfort in order to enjoy the best God had for you.

God has to change our identity before anything comes out of us. God gave Joseph a dream; it was a glimpse of his destiny.

Genesis 37:5-12--Now Joseph had a dream, and he told it to his brothers; and they hated him even more. ⁶So he said to them, "Please hear this dream which I have dreamed: ⁷There we were, binding sheaves in the field. Then behold, my sheaf arose and also stood upright; and indeed your sheaves stood all around and bowed down to my sheaf."

And his brothers said to him, "Shall you indeed reign over us? Or shall you indeed have dominion over us?" So they hated him even more for his dreams and for his words.

Then he dreamed still another dream and told it to his brothers, and said, "Look, I have dreamed another dream. And this time, the sun, the moon, and the eleven stars bowed down to me."

So he told it to his father and his brothers; and his father rebuked him and said to him, "What is this dream that you have dreamed? Shall your mother and I and your brothers indeed come to bow down to the earth before you?" ¹¹And his brothers envied him, but his father kept the matter in mind--NKJV.

That dream did not come to pass in one day. Joseph went through turbulent times before God fulfilled that dream. Your dream is true, but comes with divine testing. No pain, no gain. Glory comes after afflictions. Are you ready to endure the journey? Many people celebrate the victories of others, but they are not ready for their own. They fear the process. They want the easy way. But understand this, all things work together for good, including the pain you are going through. God has not promised us a smooth journey, but a sure, safe landing at our destiny. Accept the process of making before you enjoy your glory.

Understand your dream is in the spirit. The spiritual realm dictates to the physical realm. What you see in the spirit has more weight compared to the physical one. Therefore, focus in the spirit realm, where dreams are unfolded and become a reality.

Not all people will celebrate what God is doing in your life. God's hand upon you attracts enemies.You need to know the enemy is a tool in the hand of God. God determines how far the devil will carry out his activities in your life. You should not fear him because God is watching and planning well for you behind the scene to shame the devil.

The enemy tried to destroy Joseph, but God was working behind the curtain. There's nothing that happens which God does not know. Nothing catches God by surprise. Praise the Lord. That should give you a leverage to thank God and seek him to know His will. God never makes a mistake and will never waste any experience you are going through.

God allows tough times and the enemy's activities to move us towards destiny. God wants to receive glory through whatever we experience in life. People see the glory of God in tough times. Never fear when they come. Trust in the Lord and he will help you go through in victory.

When the three Hebrew boys were thrown in the fiery furnace, people thought that was the end of their life. But God was revealing himself through the same fire. God wanted to teach the fire a lesson. He taught the fire that He is the source of everything good existing on earth and they exists to serve His interests.

Daniel 3:16-25--Shadrach, Meshach, and Abed-Nego answered and said to the king, "O Nebuchadnezzar, we have no need to answer you in this matter. [17]If that is the case, our God whom we serve is able to deliver us from the burning fiery furnace, and He will deliver us from your hand, O king. [18]But if not, let it be known to you, O king, that we do not serve your gods, nor will we worship the gold image which you have set up."

Then Nebuchadnezzar was full of fury, and the expression on his face changed toward Shadrach, Meshach, and Abed-Nego. He spoke and commanded that they heat the furnace seven times more than it was usually heated. ²⁰And he commanded certain mighty men of valor who were in his army to bind Shadrach, Meshach, and Abed-Nego, and cast them into the burning fiery furnace. ²¹Then these men were bound in their coats, their trousers, their turbans, and their other garments, and were cast into the midst of the burning fiery furnace. ²²Therefore, because the king's command was urgent, and the furnace exceedingly hot, the flame of the fire killed those men who took up Shadrach, Meshach, and Abed-Nego. And these three men, Shadrach, Meshach, and Abed-Nego, fell down bound into the midst of the burning fiery furnace.

Then King Nebuchadnezzar was astonished; and he rose in haste and spoke, saying to his counselors, "Did we not cast three men bound into the midst of the fire?"

They answered and said to the king, "True, O king."

"Look!" he answered, "I see four men loose, walking in the midst of the fire; and they are not hurt, and the form of the fourth is like the Son of God."*--NKJV

The king could not believe his eyes—"I see four men walking in the fire". That fire won't burn you, just go through the process. Your season of victory and celebration has finally come. Take heart, the battle is of the Lord. Be in your position and never complain against the process. God is using it to glory Himself.

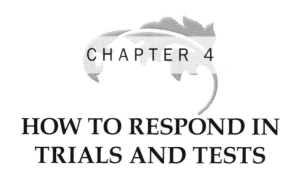

CHAPTER 4

HOW TO RESPOND IN
TRIALS AND TESTS

The enemy uses people close to us because they know us. Joseph's brothers rose against him. They planned to abort and kill his dream, but God was working behind the curtain. God is a master planner and organizer who know how to put things in place. Never worry about time and distance. God is eternal and ever present to perform His will. You need to obey and trust him. He never comes late or early; He knows the right time to intervene in your situation.

Genesis 37:18-32--Now when they saw him afar off, even before he came near them, they conspired against him to kill him. ¹⁹Then they said to one another, "Look, this dreamer is coming! ²⁰Come therefore, let us now kill him and cast him into some pit; and we shall say, 'Some wild beast has devoured him.' We shall see what will become of his dreams!"

But Reuben heard it, and he delivered him out of their hands, and said, "Let us not kill him." ²²And Reuben said to them, "Shed no blood, but cast him into this pit which is in the wilderness, and do not lay a hand on him" — that he might deliver him out of their hands, and bring him back to his father.

So it came to pass, when Joseph had come to his brothers, that they stripped Joseph of his tunic, the tunic of many colors that was on him. ²⁴Then they took him and cast him into a pit. And the pit was empty; there was no water in it.

And they sat down to eat a meal. Then they lifted their eyes and looked, and there was a company of Ishmaelites, coming from Gilead with their camels, bearing spices, balm, and myrrh, on their way to carry them down to Egypt. ²⁶So Judah said to his brothers, "What profit is there if we kill our brother and conceal his blood? ²⁷Come and let us sell him to the Ishmaelites, and let not our hand be upon him, for he is our brother and our flesh." And his brothers listened. ²⁸Then Midianite traders passed by; so the brothers pulled Joseph up and lifted him out of the pit, and sold him to the Ishmaelites for twenty shekels of silver. And they took Joseph to Egypt.

Then Reuben returned to the pit, and indeed Joseph was not in the pit; and he tore his clothes. ³⁰And he returned to his brothers and said, "The lad is no more; and I, where shall I go?"

So they took Joseph's tunic, killed a kid of the goats, and dipped the tunic in the blood. ³²Then they sent the tunic of many colors, and they brought it to their father and said, "We have found this. Do you know whether it is your son's tunic or not?" --NKJV

God was out to protect Joseph and his destiny, but the enemy was planning to abort it. Joseph was a child of destiny, so nobody could destroy his life. Joseph carried something of value. God had to stand with him to the end. Do not worry about your enemies, God knows how to deal with them.

God has hidden a treasure in us. That treasure is to serve His interests on earth. Many lives are attached to our destiny. The enemy is not happy with the anointing upon us. He knows we carry the destiny of others. We are GLORY CARRIERS.

Joseph's brothers threw him into the pit, where there was no water, but they could not take away his GIFT. People can take your clothes, but never come close to your hidden gift.

Proverb 18:16--A man's gift makes room for him and brings him before great men--AMP

God's deposit in your life cannot be taken away. You have the power either to use it or leave it dormant. Apostle Paul reminded the Roman Church that--For the gifts and the calling of God *are* irrevocable. [30]For as you were once disobedient to God, yet have now obtained mercy through their disobedience-- Romans 11:29-30, NKJV

Sharpen your gift to mature and become valuable at the market. Through the experiences Joseph was facing, God was molding him into a better person. Your gift needs constant sharpening. Some persons have gone out prematurely and created a mess.

Joseph's brothers then took his coat and dipped into the blood. To them it was a plan to trick their father, Jacob, but God saw it as a way to show forth redemption through Jesus. Blood was a sign of redemption and preservation. So Joseph was preserved towards his destiny. Understand the devil always makes mistakes which God use to fulfill His will. You may be facing hardships and trials of many kinds, but according to God, He's strengthening your inner man. Let the outward man perish, but the inward man is being renewed day by day–

Therefore we do not lose heart. Even though our outward man is perishing, yet the inward man is being renewed day by day.

¹⁷For our light affliction, which is but for a moment, is working for us a far more exceeding and eternal weight of glory, ¹⁸while we do not look at the things which are seen, but at the things which are not seen. For the things which are seen are temporary, but the things which are not seen are eternal--2ⁿᵈ Corinthians 4:18, NKJV.

God hides valuable things inside of us. We should not worry about what is going on from the outside. Joseph's brothers were against him BUT GOD WAS WORKING SOMETHING GREAT INSIDE HIS LIFE. HE NEVER MAKES A MISTAKE.

No matter what happens against you, it will definitely work for your good.

Romans 8:28--And we know that all things work together for good to those who love God, to those who are the called according to His purpose—NKJV

Joseph was put in a pit and then thrown into the prison, but still he had the **TREASURE.** There are some people in your life that will never die until they see what they have been praying for. They will see your destiny being fulfilled. Israel did not die until he saw destiny fulfilled in the life of Joseph, his beloved son. You may be going through tough times now, but at the end your dreams will speak louder than your enemies. God won't kill your enemies. He is preparing a table for you in the presence of your enemies.

Psalms 23:5-6--You prepare a table before me in the presence of my enemies; You anoint my head with oil; my cup runs over.

Surely goodness and mercy shall follow me all the days of my life; And I will dwell*in the house of the LORD-Forever--NKJV

Joseph's brothers later sold him to slavery (Ishmaelites) – for 20 shackle of silver.

Don't pray that God may kill your enemies. Let them stay to see the marvelous works of God. He is setting a table for you. So stay cool and relax as the table of celebration is being prepared. Joseph was in the same predicament. He went through hell, but he held his vision. What he saw kept him moving towards his destiny.

God passed the children of Israel through the wilderness to prepare them for Canaan. The Promised Land was a place of abundance, joy, security and everything they needed in life. God was their provider.Though God had promised them the best, they had to face tests.

Psalms 66:12--You have caused men to ride over our heads;We went through fire and through water; but You brought us out to rich fulfillment—NKJV

Joseph was tested till the word came to pass.

Psalms 105:17-19--He sent a man before them —Joseph — who was sold as a slave.

They hurt his feet with fetters, he was laid in irons.Until the time that his word came to pass, the word of the LORD tested him--NKJV

Accept the tests you are going through, they won't kill you but prepare you for your next level of glory. Allow God to work his will through you and finally you shall enjoy sweatless victories. Remember, it is for God's glory.

CHAPTER 5

PREPARING FOR THE GLORY

2 Chronicles 7:1-3

Solomon Dedicates the Temple

7 When Solomon had finished praying, fire came down from heaven and consumed the burnt offering and the sacrifices; and the glory of the LORD filled the temple. ² And the priests could not enter the house of the LORD, because the glory of the LORD had filled the LORD's house. ³ When all the children of Israel saw how the fire came down, and the glory of the LORD on the temple, they bowed their faces to the ground on the pavement, and worshiped and praised the LORD, saying:

"For He is good,
For His mercy endures forever."

Isaiah 40:3-5 (NKJV)

³ The voice of one crying in the wilderness:"Prepare the way of the LORD; Make straight in the desert A highway for our God. ⁴ Every valley shall be exalted. And every mountain and hill brought low; The crooked places shall be made straight And the rough places smooth;

⁵ The glory of the LORD shall be revealed, And all flesh shall see it together; For the mouth of the LORD has spoken."

We see the glory of God on Mt Sinai where Moses had an encounter with God. There are also a few other accounts in scripture. Glory is missing in the church today because of the lack of **desire, dedication, and denying of flesh.** When the glory of God is manifested then true revival will exist. Glory comes from the Greek word <u>"doxah"</u> meaning splendor and beauty. We have also heard it coined as "the manifested presence of God" or the magnificent beauty of God. It is God's reality in the life of mankind.

In Numbers 14:10-12, they were about to stone Caleb and Joshua after they came back with a good report that they are well able to conquer the giants in the land.

Moreover, the Lord spoke to Moses for He was angry with the people. God said, "I have shown great wonders to my people. They have seen my power and glory, but, yet, they still disobey Me and serve other gods." Moses then quickened in his spirit and began to intercede on behalf of the people asking the Lord to forgive the people. God respond to Moses and told him I will forgive them, but they will not be allowed in the promise land.

God is saying to the body of Christ that I have shown the church or the ecclesia my wonder, my power and my glory. But, they still decided to do their own thing. With their lips they say they want my glory, but their hearts are far from me. We fail to cooperate with God!

Isaiah 40:3-5 declares that we need to prepare a highway for God's glory. A highway is a straight path with many exits. On this preverbal highway, there must be changes for the glory of God to show up. When the glory shows up it makes a valley exalted, mountain a moment hill, crooked path straight and the rough places smooth.

There are four things we need to prepare for the glory.

A. Attitude and mind adjustment

We have a lot of bad attitude and negative behavior displayed in the house of God. The Bible says *"... let this mind be in you which is also in Christ Jesus."* Then in another scripture it says, *"... also think on those things that are lovely..."*

1. What are they saying about you on the job? Do they know you are saved? Are you seen as someone who gossips and undermine.
2. What are they saying about you at church? This is why the glory cannot come.
3. Can people see the glow of Jesus on you in the supermarket?
4. Are you sneaking in the drug house at night time?
5. Are you seeking help of psychics, soothsayer and witch doctors?

The glory cannot come because there is too much dabbling!

We must also change our mindset. We think too small in the Body of Christ. To understand the glory, you must think big and out of the box. We serve a huge God and His manifested presence is huge.

Psalms 24:1-2 & 7-10
the earth is the Lord and the fullness therefore...
Lift up your head oh ye gates and be ye lifted up and the king of glory...

B. Acclamation of Praise and Worship

There must be an acclamation of praise and worship in the church and among believers. The Lord has a weakness for worship. The Bible says in the book of Revelation "We were created for His presence" and "I seek such that worship, in spirit and in truth..." When you worship you cause the manifested presence of God to be.

Our Divine protection is also in the worship unto God Almighty. The reality is this, when you touch a worshiper, you just touch God. The enemy is afraid to touch a worshiper. The devil knows if he touch a worshiper. God is on His way to defend the Child of God.

Moreover, we should desire the glory cloud to rest over our lives. When the glory cloud is over your life,

1.   You and your family are safe.
2.   Your business is covered
3.   Your marriage is protected
4.   They cannot move you on the job

C. Affliction produces glory

Some of us do not want to go through nothing, but yet we want the glory. We do not want rebuke and correction, but yet we want the glory.

Bible says in 2 Corinthians 4:16-18 "16.Therefore we do not lose heart. Even though our outward man is perishing, yet the inward man is being renewed day by day. [17] For our light affliction, which is but for a moment, is working for us a far more exceeding and eternal weight of glory, [18] while we do not look at the things which are seen, but at the things which are not seen? For the things which are seen are temporary, but the things which are not seen are eternal."

Your affliction is but for a moment. It cannot be compared to the glory which shall be revealed. So, you must endure your "But for a Moment" season. Press on because it cannot be compared to what is about to come to your life.

D. Awards in the glory

There are awards in the glory. You will not experience such hardship without reward. The Bible says that you shall reap if you faith not. Some of the awards:

1. There is healing in the glory
2. The power to put everything under your feet
3. The ability to receive "Now" money in the glory
4. Guess what, the enemy cannot locate you in the glory.

In conclusion, I leave this verse of scripture with you to meditate. Psalms 63:1-5

[1] *O God, You are my God; Early will I seek You; My soul thirsts for You; My flesh longs for You In a dry and thirsty land. Where there is no water.*

[2] *So I have looked for You in the sanctuary, To see Your power and Your glory.*

[3] *Because Your loving kindness is better than life,*

[4] *Thus I will bless You while I live; I will lift up my hands in Your name.*

[5] *My soul shall be satisfied as with marrow and fatness, And my mouth shall praise You with joyful lips.*

CHAPTER 6

UNVEILING THE GLORY OF GOD

We are living in times such that we need to see the glory of God. People are hungry to see something new. I want to show you the way; the fiery furnace is where God's glory is made manifests. In this place, God cannot share His glory with anyone. Jacob was left alone and he wrestled with the Angel of the Lord until daybreak. Jesus was left alone in the Garden of Gethsemane while His trusted disciples comfortably slept. Furnace of trials is a place of separation and refining. God is bringing you out from your past and ushering you into your destiny.

Many people want to see God's glory, but they are not ready to walk with God through the place of refining and testing. Remember, Glory is manifested in the furnace.

Isaiah 48:10-11--Behold, I have refined you, but not as silver;I have tested you in the furnace of affliction.For My own sake, for My own sake, I will do it;For how should My name be profaned?And I will not give My glory to another--NKJV

If you are not willing to go with God into the fire of trials and tests, you won't see His glory.The children of Israel could not possess the Promised Land with Egyptian mentality. God took them through the wilderness. Wilderness was a process to sieve bad elements from them. Wilderness revealed what was hidden in them. God took them there for a purpose because he was preparing them for what was ahead. Are you going through your wilderness? Don't die in your wilderness; let your wilderness deal with your character.

Fiery trials should bring you down on your knees, and make you humble so that you can tap into the power of God. There is power in prayer. The three Hebrew boys were thrown into the fiery furnace and fell down bound. The Bible says later they became loosed from their shackles. The fourth man appeared in the fiery furnace and preserved them from destruction. God is with you even in the fire. He will never leave you or forsake you. Trust in the Lord with all your heart and lean not to your own understanding.

God wants to use you after going through the process because many people are connected to your destiny. God's way of preparing a vessel is different from the way we think. Some people expect quick results which do not last. Going through trials and tests may seem like a failure and foolishness, but to God, it is worth it. You learn some lessons from that school which Bible school cannot deliver. Tears that you shed in the secret which people don't know about are rewarded by the Lord because you have passed the tests.

Look at this practical example, the devil wanted worship, but the three Hebrew boys said no, it cannot happen. We all know that worship belongs to God, the Maker of heaven and the earth. It was a test of faith and conviction to the Hebrew boys. Ultimately, they made it. You shall make it through the journey though it may be rough and tough.

Daniel 3:19-27--Then Nebuchadnezzar was full of fury, and the expression on his face changed toward Shadrach, Meshach, and Abed-Nego. He spoke and commanded that they heat the furnace seven times more than it was usually heated. [20]And he commanded certain mighty men of valor who were in his army to bind Shadrach, Meshach, and Abed-Nego, and cast them into the burning fiery furnace. [21]Then these men were bound in their coats, their trousers, their turbans, and their other garments, and were cast into the midst of the burning fiery furnace. [22]Therefore, because the king's command was urgent, and the furnace exceedingly hot, the flame of the fire killed those men who took up Shadrach, Meshach, and Abed-Nego.

And these three men, Shadrach, Meshach, and Abed-Nego, fell down bound into the midst of the burning fiery furnace.

Then King Nebuchadnezzar was astonished; and he rose in haste and spoke, saying to his counselors, "Did we not cast three men bound into the midst of the fire?"

They answered and said to the king, "True, O king."

"Look!" he answered, "I see four men loose, walking in the midst of the fire; and they are not hurt, and the form of the fourth is like the Son of God."*

Then Nebuchadnezzar went near the mouth of the burning fiery furnace and spoke, saying, "Shadrach, Meshach, and Abed-Nego, servants of the Most High God, come out, and come here." Then Shadrach, Meshach, and Abed-Nego came from the midst of the fire. [27]And the satraps, administrators, governors, and the king's counselors gathered together, and they saw these men on whose bodies the fire had no power; the hair of their head was

not singed nor were their garments affected, and the smell of fire
was not on them--NKJV

Meshach, Shadrach and Abednego were not willing to bow before
the golden idol. The King Nebuchadnezzar did everything to the
boys. He took away their diet and gave them the diet of idols. He
also took away their Hebrew names – Hananiah, Mischael, and
Azariah. Changing their diets and names did not affect them.
They had seen the true God, so betraying their conviction was not
an option. They decided to go the hard way of the fiery furnace.
They took the side of God as recipient of true worship.

BE A WORSHIPER

You cannot touch a worshipper. When you dare touch a worshiper,
you meet God of the worshiper. That is why I encourage you to be
a worshiper. It takes you deep in God where He reveals Himself
to you in a new way. You move from shallow worship to true
worship that enhances your spiritual growth. True Worshipers
acquire strength from God who takes them through trials and
temptations. God loves worship and therefore he guards his own
from danger and attacks of the enemy because they have a place
in his heart.

Genesis 22:4-6--On the third day Abraham looked up and saw
the place in the distance. ⁵He said to his servants, "Stay here
with the donkey while I and the boy go over there. We will
worship and then we will come back to you."--NIV

Abraham was a worshiper of the living God. God fulfilled His
promise by giving him a son and later demanded that Abraham
should give him as a sacrifice. Abraham did not waver in faith
as the Bible records in the above passage; he went to Mount

Moriah, to worship. There is power in worship. If believers can understand the power behind worship, most of our problems would be solved. You cannot be a worshiper and you life remain the same. God loves worship because he deserves it. He is the source of our being, success and sustenance. We cannot do without him. The Bible says in Him we live, we move and have are very existence.

Trials and tests come to those who worship and those who do not. But the advantage that worshipers have, is that God gives them His grace to go through. God's grace is what makes life colorful. You may be in trials, but you see them as tools of refreshments. The place where God reveals His glory in a new dimension to the willing mind. Are you ready for that?

Fiery trials of life have no power over you unless God permits. So you need not to fear when they come. Remember God cannot permit something that is greater than your faith. God says in His word, *"I will never leave you nor forsake you"*. His word is final, the anchor of our faith to remain still in afflictions. Afflictions produce glory.

The Greek word for glory is "doxah" which may also mean splendor. IT IS IN THE FIERY FURNACE THAT YOU SEE SPLENDOR. People who go there by God's will always reveal the glory of God.

The enemy can take you through hardships and mock at you. What will you do? Hang on the word of God. God is able to deliver you from any situation which the devil may have put you in. Understand this, the war between God and Satan is worship. The enemy uses contrary situations to make people bow before him. True worship is directed to God. He deserves it. Do not allow the enemy to deceive you.

Trials and temptations are part of life. Just endure and you are going to see the glory of God. God can also use fiery trial to get rid of unwanted elements out of your life. You cannot see the glory of God in a new dimension with your former state. People see the glory of God when you go through fiery trials and still stand to praise the Lord.

Ephesians 3:20-4:1--Now to Him who is able to do exceedingly abundantly above all that we ask or think, according to the power that works in us, [21]to Him be glory in the church by Christ Jesus to all generations, forever and ever. Amen--NKJV

The Bible says, God is able to do exceedingly abundantly above all that we ask. That guarantees our rest and victory in Him. When trials come, we have a shield to run to. When the enemy attacks our faith, we use the weapons of our warfare to fight him because we are standing on the firm foundation that cannot be shaken.

Shift your focus from what is invisible and turn to the invisible. Physical things are transient, spiritual things are permanent. Faith stands on the invisible, what God has said.

Psalms 46:1-3--God is our refuge and strength, a very present help in trouble.Therefore we will not fear, even though the earth be removed and though the mountains be carried into the midst of the sea; though its waters roar and be troubled, thoughthe mountains shake with its swelling—NKJV

God is your refuge and a present help in every situation. You are standing on the rock of ages; that cannot be shaken. That place gives you stability and focus to remain standing when other things are tumbling down. How I pray and desire that believers may find a better place to dwell in God where you are kept safe and secure.

When God calls you in His presence, be still. When you are there, everything falls in place. Fear, worries, anxieties and every negative emotion recede in the horizon, leaving you unaffected because you know whom you trust.

Psalms 46:10--Be still, and know that I am God; I will be exalted among the nations, I will be exalted in the earth!--NKJV

God has promised you, be still and see His faithfulness. Do not panic. Do not move from your position. Promotion comes after you have gone through the fire.

Psalms 75:6--Promotion comes from God. Sometimes it may come through the fire of trials. But stand firm. God is faithful to see you through until His will is accomplished in your life.

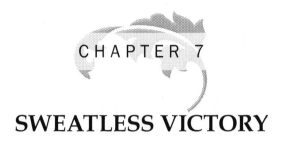

CHAPTER 7

SWEATLESS VICTORY

Jehoshaphat was a worshiper of the living God. He led Judah to the paths of worship and the land enjoyed maximum peace and tranquility. People enjoyed the blessings of God and continued to prosper. Whenever people turn to God, the heavens respond accordingly. God is calling us to the place of worship to encounter Him in a new dimension. This was the situation in Judah where the King brought the entire land to seek God.

Many times troubles, hardships and crisis force us in the presence of God. This should not be the way. Worship is the willingness of the heart. No one should force you to worship.

King Jehoshaphat and Judah worshipped God in spirit and in truth. Things went on smoothly because of that environment. The devil was not happy with the prosperity of Judah; he engineered a scheme to deal with them. The enemy is not happy with our worship. He tends to interfere and try to pollute it because it makes him sick and mad.

From the beginning, after the Lucifer (devil) rebel against God, the devil desires the worship that belongs to God. He tried to convince Jesus to worship him and the whole world with its pleasure would be at his beckon. But Jesus saw beyond that because He knew worship is for and of God. Can you bow to the world and give worship to the enemy? Your faith would be tested to the core. Meshach, Shadrach and Abednego were thrown into the fiery furnace because they refused to bow before the golden image. God saw their conviction and he rescued them.

King Jehoshaphat was in the same predicament. The enemy saw the King's determination and willingness to worship God that made him mad about it. The Bible records that King Jehoshaphat was a God seeker.

2 Chronicles 20:3-4--And Jehoshaphat feared, and set himself to seek the Lord, and proclaimed a fast throughout all Judah. ⁴So Judah gathered together to ask help from the Lord; and from all the cities of Judah they came to seek the Lord--NKJV

Ammon, Moab and Mount Seir came against King Jehoshaphat in battle. They want to frustrate his efforts and destroy his kingdom completely so that the people may forget the true God. Whatever the devil does is to interfere with our worship. Worship makes Satan mad. It inflicts pain and makes the enemy confused. Let nothing stop your worship. Worship is the key to know God. You encounter God at the place of worship.

Never allow your priorities to be misplaced and given to other things. What we see is transient; it is passing away like a shadow. We are commanded to focus on the invisible. Eternal things are valuable compared to the physical. You should know that very well to stop the enemy from prevailing against you. Remember our battle is not carnal, but spiritual. We begin from the spiritual realm and then affect the physical world. That is the right way to go.

2 Corinthians 10:3-6--For though we live in the world, we do not wage war as the world does. ⁴The weapons we fight with are not the weapons of the world. On the contrary, they have divine power to demolish strongholds. ⁵We demolish arguments and every pretension that sets itself up against the knowledge of God, and we take captive every thought to make it obedient to Christ. ⁶And we will be ready to punish every act of disobedience, once your obedience is complete--NIV

Remember your warfare is not carnal, but spiritual. If you know your position, the enemy cannot dislodge you. You are better equipped to deal with him just the way King Jehoshaphat faced his enemies. Most people think we are fighting against flesh and blood. So they see people as real enemies. The enemy can use people to fight us, but that should not distract our attention. We know which enemy we are dealing with and so we use spiritual weapons to fight him. That way, we are guaranteed the victory. I pray that God give you understanding in the name of Jesus.

King Jehoshaphat knew his God and positioned himself in spite of the enemies impending attack. He went to the temple to seek the Lord. He began from the right place which is seeking the Lord for divine intervention. Your priority should focus on God first before other things fall in place. The devil does not mind if you run your life without God. He knows very well you will reach your end and give up. The right way is to seek God. King Jehoshaphat led Judah to seek the God of Abraham, Isaac and Jacob.

2 Chronicles 20:5-8--Then Jehoshaphat stood in the assembly of Judah and Jerusalem, in the house of the Lord, *before the new court, ⁶and said: "O* Lord *God of our fathers, are You not God in heaven, and do You not rule over all the kingdoms of the nations, and in Your hand is there not power and might, so that no one is able to withstand You? ⁷Are You not our God, who drove out the inhabitants of this land before Your people Israel, and gave it to the descendants of Abraham Your friend forever? –NKJV*

How did King Jehoshaphat make it? He positioned himself with the rest of Judah. So the number one thing was to take the right position.

1. Position

Position has to do with your location, posture in the spirit, and being strategically placed. Take your place where God is directing you in the battle field. If you leave your place you will not experience and enjoy your victory.

The Bible says in Ephesians 6:10--Finally, my brethren, be strong in the Lord and in the power of His might. ¹¹Put on the whole armor of God, that you may be able to stand against the wiles of the devil. ¹²For we do not wrestle against flesh and blood, but against principalities, against powers, against the rulers of the darkness of this age,*against spiritual hosts of wickedness in the heavenly places. ¹³Therefore take up the whole armor of God, that you may be able to withstand in the evil day, and having done all, to stand—NKJV

To win any battle in the spirit, you should be strategically positioned. The weapons we use against the enemy are mighty through God to the pulling down of strongholds. But our position matters a lot. When you are in your place, those weapons do a lot of damage in the camp of the enemy. That is why Apostle Paul said, "be strong in the Lord". Position yourself properly. It is not as if the enemy is stronger and has better weapons than we do. We, as children of God, just fail to pick up and use the weapons that God has given us to combat the enemy.

The devil will try to kill and abort your destiny. He is not happy with your stand in faith and achievement of prosperity in the kingdom of God. The enemy's mission is to kill, steal and to destroy. Remember, when you defeat your enemy, he will reinforce to counter attack. Never celebrate for long and leave your place.

One of the greatest weapons the enemy uses is FEAR. Fear is the strength of the enemy. When you conquer fear, you have won all battles because God operates in the environment of faith. According to the KJV Dictionary Fear is a painful emotion or passion excited by the expectation of evil. The word **FEAR stands for Friction Exist Appearing Real**. It is just a smoke screen created by the enemy.

Jehoshaphat conquered fear.

Psalms 125:1-2--Those who trust in the Lord *are like Mount Zion, which cannot be moved, but abides forever. As the mountains surround Jerusalem, so the* Lord *surrounds His people from this time forth and forever--NKJV*

God admonishes us, not to fear.

Fear and faith cannot exist in the same place. Fear will cause you to be conquered. So, we must conquer fear. Fear and faith comes by hearing either positive or negative information. The question is what are you hearing? You rise in faith or become the devil's play boy by listening to his information. The word of God is the source of true faith. Adhere to the word of God. Let your spirit be nourished with the word of God and you shall excel in the things of God.

Let me tell you, fear opens the door to the enemy's attacks.
Fear opens the gate to diseases and sickness.

Fear is the doorway to failures.

Job 3:25--For the thing I greatly feared has come upon me, and what I dreaded has happened to me—NKJV

Whatever happened to Job is as a result of fear. Fear is a child of the devil, never gives it a place. You need to conquer fear by standing in faith, just like King Jehoshaphat. Fear threatened his existence and the people of Judah but they turned to God in faith. That step gave them victory over fear. The Bible evidences that fear is not of God because in the word it says God has not given you the spirit of fear, but of power love and a sound mind (2 Timothy 1:7).

2. Prayer

Prayer is another powerful weapon that a child of God possesses. We ought to have a consistent prayer life. The Bible says men ought always to pray.

2 Chronicles 20:5-13--Then Jehoshaphat stood in the assembly of Judah and Jerusalem, in the house of the LORD, before the new court, ⁶and said: "O LORD God of our fathers, areYou not God in heaven, and do You not rule over all the kingdoms of the nations, and in Your hand is there not power and might, so that no one is able to withstand You? ⁷Are You not our God, who drove out the inhabitants of this land before Your people Israel, and gave it to the descendants of Abraham Your friend forever? ⁸And they dwell in it, and have built You a sanctuary in it for Your name, saying, ⁹If disaster comes upon us — sword, judgment, pestilence, or famine — we will stand before this temple and in Your presence (for Your name is in this temple), and cry out to You in our affliction, and You will hear and save.'

38

And now, here are the people of Ammon, Moab, and Mount Seir — whom You would not let Israel invade when they came out of the land of Egypt, but they turned from them and did not destroy them — ¹¹here they are, rewarding us by coming to throw us out of Your possession which You have given us to inherit. ¹²O our God, will You not judge them? For we have no power against this great multitude that is coming against us; nor do we know what to do, but our eyes are upon You." Now all Judah, with their little ones, their wives, and their children, stood before the LORD--NKJV

Jehoshaphat dealt with his fears by prayer. There is proof and power in prayer. Believers need to know the secret of staying in God's presence. We prevail by God's grace, so we need His presence to strengthen us. I am praying that believers should discover the power behind prayer. Never allow your work or anything to take the place of God. Let prayer be your priority.

Sometimes it is important to add fasting to your prayer. There are things which fasting can deal with them. Prayer and fasting reinforces you and you are given strategies to deal with the enemy.

Isaiah 58:6-9--"Is this not the fast that I have chosen: to loose the bonds of wickedness, to undo the heavy burdens, to let the oppressed go free, and that you break every yoke? Is it not to share your bread with the hungry, and that you bring to your house the poor who are cast out; when you see the naked, that you cover him, and not hide yourself from your own flesh? Then your light shall break forth like the morning, your healing shall spring forth speedily, and your righteousness shall go before you; The glory of the LORD shall be your rear guard.Then you shall call, and the LORD will answer; you shall cry, and He will say, 'Here I am.'--NKJV

Prophet Isaiah gives us the power behind fasting. In the above passage, several effects of fasting are mentioned. You should set aside time to fast to see God in new dimensions. We should object and get tired of living an average, normal mediocre and ordinary life. Get on your knees and cry to God, you will encounter new realms of the spirit that ushers you to a new season of your life.

Power of fasting

- Loose the bands of wickedness
- Undo the heavy burdens
- Set the captives free
- Empower you with an anointing to break every yoke over your life.
- Your light will break forth announcing your new season.
- The Glory of God will be made manifest in your own life.
- The answer to your prayers will come with great speed.

2 Chronicles 20:14-17--Then the Spirit of the LORD came upon Jahaziel the son of Zechariah, the son of Benaiah, the son of Jeiel, the son of Mattaniah, a Levite of the sons of Asaph, in the midst of the assembly. ¹⁵And he said, "Listen, all you of Judah and you inhabitants of Jerusalem, and you, King Jehoshaphat! Thus says the LORD to you:'Do not be afraid nor dismayed because of this great multitude, for the battle is not yours, but God's. ¹⁶Tomorrow go down against them. They will surely come up by the Ascent of Ziz, and you will find them at the end of the brook before the Wilderness of Jeruel. YOU WILL NOT NEED TO FIGHT IN THIS BATTLE.POSITION YOURSEVES, STAND STILL AND SEE THE SALVATION OF THE LORD, who is with you, O Judah and Jerusalem!' Do not fear or be dismayed; tomorrow go out against them, for the LORD is with you."--NKJV

One word from God changes everything. God gave His word through the prophet and Jehoshaphat heard it. It brought relief and calmness in the whole multitude. I said, faith comes by hearing the word of God. Be eager to hear His voice through the word; it is the anchor to your soul. No fear can settle in your heart when you allow the word of God to dominate your life. Hearing the voice of God brings healing and gives you Divine direction.

The word came and the atmosphere changed -"**position yourself and stand still**". God is telling you stand still in the midst of your challenges. Never move an inch from the place of trust. Your position matters a lot in the realm of the spirit.

Doctor's report can lie.
People's opinions are limited.
The economy may not be stable.

- Only the word of God can turn scarcity into abundance.
- One word from God will open doors that have been closed.
- One word from God can turn mourning to rejoicing.

The centurion believed the power of spoken word. He asked Jesus to speak a word and a miracle happened that day. Stay in the word that is the place of your breakthrough—

Matthew 8:8-13--The centurion answered and said, "Lord, I am not worthy that You should come under my roof. But only speak a word, and my servant will be healed. ⁹For I also am a man under authority, having soldiers under me. And I say to this one, 'Go,' and he goes; and to another, 'Come,' and he comes; and to my servant, 'Do this,' and he does it."

When Jesus heard it, He marveled, and said to those who followed, "Assuredly, I say to you, I have not found such great faith, not even in Israel! ¹¹And I say to you that many will come from east and west, and sit down with Abraham, Isaac, and Jacob in the kingdom of heaven. ¹²But the sons of the kingdom will be cast out into outer darkness. There will be weeping and gnashing of teeth." ¹³Then Jesus said to the centurion, "Go your way; and as you have believed, so let it be done for you." And his servant was healed that same hour--NKJV.

When you receive the word of God and believe it, you are already on your way to receive a miracle. Remember, God watches his word to perform it - Jeremiah 1:12.

All those who received the word and believed it, their situations changed. Peter the fisherman in Luke 5:1- responded to the word and he had net breaking experience. The man, who had stayed for 38 years at the pool of Bethesda, got his miracle because the word of healing came—John 5:1-8. Now it is your turn of healing, deliverance, restoration and salvation even as you receive this knowledge. Prepare and move in faith because the water of your miracle has been stirred up.

3. Praise

Praise is another potent weapon. This weapon literally sends the enemy into confusion. He is wondering how is it that the enemy has bombarded you and you still have your right mind and you are still praising God.

2 Chronicles 20:18-19--And Jehoshaphat bowed his head with his face to the ground, and all Judah and the inhabitants of Jerusalem bowed before the LORD, worshiping the LORD. ¹⁹Then the Levites of the children of the Kohathites and of the children of the Korahites stood up to praise the LORD God of Israel with voices loud and high--NKJV

After taking his position in the presence of God, he moved further to another level of praise. Jehoshaphat appointed the praise team to go to the frontline of the battle. Judah means "praise."

Praise is powerful. When you touch Judah (worshiper), you meet the God of Praise. The Bible says that after singers had praised the Lord, He sent an ambush against the enemy and they smote each other. Praises confuses the enemy and cause him to lose all composure. Praise God from Zion!

Praise in Hebrew means "Yadah", is the lifting of hands as sign of victory.

Psalms 8:2--Out of the mouth of babes and nursing infants, you have ordained strength, Because of Your enemies, that You may silence the enemy and the avenger—NKJV

God ordains praise in the lips of the children. He paralyzes the enemy. Paul and Silas prayed as the Bible says in Acts 16:25 and then engaged in another gear of PRAISE, the enemy was confused, and he had no choice, but to release them. The chains were loosed; the gates were opened. Paul and his companion Silas were released from prison. What is it that is bothering your spirit? Turn that thing to praise.

There is power when you praise God with all your heart. Understand this, God dwells in the praises of His people - Psalms 22:3. When God shows up, power is released and things begin to work. Burdens are lifted. Sickness and diseases are destroyed. The captives are made free to fulfill their purpose.

2 Chronicles 20:22-24--Now when they began to sing and to praise, the LORD set ambushes against the people of Ammon, Moab, and Mount Seir, who had come against Judah; and they were defeated. ²³***For the people of Ammon and Moab stood up against the inhabitants of Mount Seir to utterly kill and destroy them. And when they had made an end of the inhabitants of Seir, they helped to destroy one another.***

So when Judah came to a place overlooking the wilderness, they looked toward the multitude; and there were their dead bodies, fallen on the earth. No one had escaped--NKJV

None of the enemy escaped. They were all dead, leaving behind a great spoil for the children of Israel to possess. That is your season of celebration. What the enemy planned against you, God is turning around for your favor. Right where you are, just begin to celebrate the goodness of the Lord.

4. Prosperity

God prospers His people. It is the will of God for you to prosper. Poverty is not humility, it is a curse. Jesus redeemed us from all curses, so you have all the reason to enjoy God's blessings. The Bible says the children of Judah gathered the spoil for three days. God had given them victory over their enemies and also they had valuable goods left behind by the enemy to carry home. God is so great that He prepares a table before you in the presence of your enemies. Celebrate the Lord's goodness and faithfulness. Jehoshaphat and Judah had more than enough. We serve a God of more than enough. A child of God should never accept to live below the standard that God has marked.

Refuse to be trapped in the same place forever. You need to be mad against your status in life and say enough is enough, "I am entering my next season of prosperity'".

2 Chronicles 20:25--When Jehoshaphat and his people came to take away their spoil, they found among them an abundance of valuables on the dead bodies,*and precious jewelry, which they stripped off for themselves, more than they could carry away; and they were three days gathering the spoil because there was so much--NKJV

King Jehoshaphat and Judah had something to celebrate. They trusted in God and gave Him all the praise. God moved in their situation and fought against their enemies. The Bible says when they reached where their enemies were, they found dead bodies. May God fight for you.The same thing happened in the book of Esther about Mordecai. The king Xerxes gave Mordecai what he had given Haman. The place where you cried, God will turn your ashes into beauty and give your oil of joy for mourning. Your mourning will change to dancing—Psalms 30:5

The same place where the enemy came to attack Judah became a waterloo for them. In the same place where they put the shackles on you, you shall be set free. In the same place where they said it will end, God will prosper you. In the same place where they kept you down, you shall receive your promotion. I decree and declare, "In the same place." The enemies were ashamed and defeated because God gave them SWEAT LESS VICTORY. That is your portion in Jesus name.

Isaiah 55:11--So shall My word be that goes forth from My mouth; it shall not return to Me void, but it shall accomplish what I please, and it shall prosper in the thing for which I sent it--NKJV

God's word must prosper. Nothing can hinder its potent power. What has God spoken over your life? Hold that word and run with it. Though it tarries, at the end, it shall speak for you.

CHAPTER 8

DISMANTLE THE WORKS
OF THE DEVIL

The devil is a real enemy. His mandate is as in John 10:10 which is to kill, steal and to destroy. Jesus said, "But I have come that you might have life and have it more abundantly." As we know, one third of the angels along with Lucifer decided to rebel against God in the beginning. This resulted with the now devil and his demons being kicked out of heaven.

Jesus came to destroy the works of the devil.

The reason that Jesus appeared was to reconcile us to God. In 1 John 3:8b we find these words *"The reason the Son of God appeared was to destroy the works of the Devil."*

The demonic activity and the horrible and destructive things that Satan and his demons attempt to do to those who bear the image of God is a reality. It is not a myth. The devil and his demons are real and must be dismantled and annihilated.

According to the dictionary, the word "destroy" means to loose, to unbind, to unravel, or to dissolve. Thus, Satan's works are conceived as chains that bind us, which Jesus now breaks. Jesus came to undo and to dissolve the enemy's efforts. What are Satan's "works"?

Spiritually, he blinds the minds of unbelievers so they are not able to see and believe the gospel.

Morally, he entices many persons to sin and to make some walk contrary to the Word and the instructions of God.

Physically, he inflicts disease and the spirit of infirmity on many believers. The devil also seeks to destroy those who bear the image of God.

Intellectually, he seduces many to perform evil acts and deceives some to walk on the wrong path.

And *Emotionally*, many are distraught in our thoughts and emotion. Some even want to give up on life. But the devil is a liar! You shall live and not die to declare the works of the Lord in Jesus name.

Jesus destroyed the works of the Devil when he successfully resisted the Devil's temptations. He also delivered people and drove out demons and set people free from their bondage to the devil.

Second, Jesus also destroyed the works of the Devil by means of his death. Satan has come to try to vitiate or spoil God's glory. Jesus has come to vindicate it. Satan seeks to undermine God's glory. Jesus aimed to uphold it. At His death, He went down and got the keys of death, hell and the grave. The devil was defeated. "O death where is thy sting, O grave where is thy victory?" 1 Corinthians 15:55

Satan's aim is to keep men and women in their sin, under its penalty, held in bondage to its power, suffering mental and emotional defeat from its guilty accusations. Insofar as Christ's death secured redemption from sin and its guilt, Satan has suffered defeat. Colossians 2:14-15 says **¹⁴ having wiped out the handwriting of requirements that was against us, which was contrary to us. And He has taken it out of the way, having nailed it to the cross. ¹⁵ Having disarmed principalities and powers, He made a public spectacle of them, triumphing over them in it.**

We have the victory of Christ over the demonic and the authority and power is ours if we believe, if we take our stand in the name and authority of the risen Christ, *"for he who is in you is greater than he who is in the world"* (1 John 4:4).

He has also empowered us to conquer the devil and his imps in our daily lives. We must understand how they are structured. This is an organized regime. They do not skip rank and file. The ranks are principalities, powers, rulers of darkness and wickedness in high places as found in Ephesians 6:12 which declare **For we do not wrestle against flesh and blood, but against principalities, against powers, against the rulers of the darkness of this age, against spiritual hosts of wickedness in the high places.**

We are able to destroy the works of the enemy through the following:

- ❖ Prayer
- ❖ Praise & worship
- ❖ Fasting
- ❖ Declaring the Word of God
- ❖ And calling on the powerful name of Jesus. Philippians 2:9-10 says that **the Lord highly exalted "His son and**

gave Him a name that is above all names. That at the name of Jesus every knee shall bow of those in heaven and of those on the earth and of those under the earth.

You must learn how to use God's power to free your life from Satan's control. You must thoroughly understand the strategies of the enemy and learn to apply God's power to every area of bondage or confusion you may be experiencing from the devil.

Authority is your power from God. It is your ability to have influence over someone or something. The devil has no authority over you. Psalms 8:6 says that all things have been placed under your feet.

We must walk after the spirit and not mind the things of the flesh.

1 John 4:1-3 (KJV) **says, Beloved, believe not every spirit, but try the spirits whether they are of God: because many false prophets are gone out into the world. ² Hereby know ye the Spirit of God: Every spirit that confess that Jesus Christ is come in the flesh is of God: ³ And every spirit that do not confess that Jesus Christ is come in the flesh is not of God: and this is that spirit of antichrist, whereof ye have heard that it should come; and even now already is it in the world.**

1 Timothy 4:1 (NKJV) says **now the Spirit expressly says that in latter times some will depart from the faith, giving heed to deceiving spirits and doctrines of demons.**

Let me share, in closing, some scriptures that you can pray and use against the enemy to dismantle his works.

➢ Spirit of Bondage – Read Romans 8:15
➢ Spirit of Divination – Read Acts 16:16

49

- ➢ Spirit of sleep Isaiah – Read 29:10
- ➢ A broken spirit – Read Proverbs 17:22
- ➢ Spirits that compel men to do diabolical things – Read Malachi 3:5
- ➢ Spirits who corrupt men to negotiate with the souls through witchcraft, enchantment and magic Ezekiel 13:18-19

Once you have dismantled the works of darkness, you must endeavor to keep your freedom by doing the following:

1. Destroy all occult objects from your surroundings. Keep your house clean. Acts 19:18-19 says **And many who had believed came confessing and telling their deeds. ¹⁹ Also, many of those who had practiced magic brought their books together and burned *them* in the sight of all. And they counted up the value of them, and *it* totaled fifty thousand *pieces* of silver.**

2. Have a consistent prayer life. Jude 20 says, **But you, beloved, building yourselves up on your most holy faith, praying in the Holy Spirit,**

3. Study the Word of God daily and develop a relationship with the Almighty God. 2 Timothy 2:15 says, **Be diligent to present yourself approved to God, a worker who does not need to be ashamed, rightly dividing the word of truth.**

4. Guard your mind and thoughts. Philippians 4:6-7 says, **Be anxious for nothing, but in everything by prayer and supplication, with thanksgiving, let your requests be made known to God; ⁷ and the peace of God, which surpasses all understanding, will guard your hearts and minds through Christ Jesus..**

5. <u>Confess your deliverance and denounce the works of the devil</u>. Joel 2:32 says, **And it shall come to pass** *That* **whoever calls on the name of the** Lord **Shall be saved. For in Mount Zion and in Jerusalem there shall be deliverance, As the** Lord **has said, Among the remnant whom the** Lord **calls..**

6. <u>Get rid of resentment, unforgiveness and hatred towards other people</u> Mark 11:25-26 says, **And whenever you stand praying, if you have anything against anyone, forgive him that your Father in heaven may also forgive you your trespasses.** [26] **But if you do not forgive, neither will your Father in heaven forgive your trespasses.** Psalms 66:18 says, **If I regard iniquity in my heart, The Lord will not hear.**

Commit your life totally to the Lord and your life will be a fruitful one. You have the power to dismantle the works of the devil. Exercise you Divine power and live a life of freedom in Jesus name.

For this power to be effective, we must ensure that your walk with the Lord is right and also ensure that your love walk with your brothers and sisters are in order. This will allow the Lord to reign and have free course in your affairs and everything that concerns you.

PRAYER OF VICTORY

Defeating Satanic Network –

- When there is a network of evil surrounding you.
- When you feel as if the whole world is against you.

The Lord is a man of war and would muster His superior forces to destroy any satanic network that is working against you.

Job 5:12 says, **"He disappointed the devices of the crafty, so that their hands cannot perform their enterprise."** The enemy is disappointed because his plot and plan against you did not work.

Romans 8:31 **If God be for you, then who can be against you? What shall separate you from the love of God?**

With the anointing on my life, I say this prayer for you:

- I command all demonic contracts be cast into the fire in the name of Jesus.
- Let every demonic trap set against your life be shattered in the name of Jesus.
- All organized demonic plots against you are pulled down.
- I command all your pictures that are being used in the demonic realm to be burned to pieces and have no effect in the name of Jesus.
- I plead the blood over your food, over your emotion and over your health. Let the blood prevail in Jesus name.

- I dismantle every spirit of oppression and depression even every suicidal thought be destroyed in the name of Jesus.
- My Lord, My God raise up Godly intercessors to pray for my brother, to pray for my sisters.
- Father, let every dormant spirit arise. The kingdom suffers violence, but the believer must take it back by force.
- I cast down the spirit of fear and bondage in Jesus name.
- I reject all uncontrollable crying, heaviness, regrets, bitterness and resentment in the name of Jesus.
- You are VICTORIOUS! You are a WINNER! You are strong as a lion!
- Father, do not take their life until their ministry has been fulfilled in Jesus name. Amen!

If you feel a sense of victory and you felt the power exude from this prayer, go ahead and give my God praise. Let me hear your VICTORY ROAR!

CONCLUSION

Every believer must have a level of buoyancy just like a ball. The more you push a ball down in the water, once released, the higher the ball shoots into the air. The more you are pushed down in life, ostracize and told that you are nothing, the higher God will allow you to rise. The Lord will make the enemy out to be a liar and cancel every negative word spoken over your life.

You may wonder at your life and think as if God is not concerned with you. Listen to me; God's plans for you are real. His plans never fail. They are reserved for His children. Are you one of His children? Are you really born again?

I want to help you here. Going through hard times without God is in vain. There is no reward for you. I suggest to you, this is the time to make right with God.

The Bible says in Romans 10:8-13--But what does it say? "The word is near you, in your mouth and in your heart"*(that is, the word of faith which we preach): ⁹that if you confess with your mouth the Lord Jesus and believe in your heart that God has raised Him from the dead, you will be saved. ¹⁰For with the heart one believes unto righteousness, and with the mouth confession is made unto salvation. ¹¹For the Scripture says, "Whoever believes on Him will not be put to shame."* ¹²For there is no distinction between Jew and Greek, for the same Lord over all is rich to all who call upon Him. ¹³For "whoever calls on the name of the LORD shall be saved."* ---NKJV

Jesus is the way, the truth and life. Allow him into your heart and he will stand with you in your trials. God's grace will carry you in times of difficulties. I am praying for you.

I want to assure you, Jesus is the best option you can have in life. Any journey you take towards your destiny, you have a guarantee of safe arrival. Maybe now you are contemplating to throw down your towel and quit because life has given you hard blows. But that is the way of defeat.

To others, it seems like you are a loser and a gone case. They have predicted that you will never amount to anything. That devil is a liar and the truth is not in him. Open your eyes and see, it is not a gone case. Jesus can open a brand new page for you. Just allow him in your life. He met several people in the Bible and changed their story. You are next in the line. Do not give up. Do not develop ulcers. This is the time of your change. Accept Jesus in your life and see the desired changes. He is the master physician with wisdom to attend to your deepest needs.

If you have not accepted the Lord Jesus into your heart, then your life is incomplete. Below is a prayer to help you to get saved and begin experience the abundant life.

Confess this prayer from your heart,

"Lord Jesus, I repent of my sins and confess them before you. Forgive me and cleanse me by your precious blood. Come into my heart and save my life. Thank you Jesus for saving my life. Write my name in the book of life. Grant me today the grace to live for you. I confess this prayer believing in my heart you are Lord and Savior of my life, in Jesus name I pray", Amen.

Printed in the United States
By Bookmasters